Contents

Edexcel GCSE Introduction

Edexcel GCSE is the world's most popular international qualification for 14 to 16 year olds. It is recognized by leading universities and employers worldwide, and is an international passport to progression and success. Developed over 25 years ago, it is tried, tested and trusted by schools worldwide. This syllabus is designed for learners who are learning Mandarin Chinese as a foreign language. The aim is to develop an ability to use the language effectively for purposes of practical communication. The course is based on the linked language skills of listening, reading, speaking and writing, and these are built on as learners' progress through their studies. There are four papers:

Edexcel GCSE Chinese 5CN01-1F Listening - Foundation Tier

Edexcel GCSE Chinese 5CN01-1H Listening - Higher Tier

Edexcel GCSE Chinese 5CN03-3F Reading - Foundation Tier

Edexcel GCSE Chinese 5CN03-3H Reading - Higher Tier

Preface

PREFACE

Our Edexcel GCSE Chinese Intensive Revision Reading is based on the past year papers with our in-depth explanations. Each past paper will have 3 related products:

1. Intensive Revision PDF Book - A Quick Reference to past
2. Online Quiz - A Quick Reference to past Exam Papers
3. Intensive Revision Video Course - Examination Skills, Tips and Guide

All vocabularies in these courses are given the Best English Translation for better understanding based our years' experience in HSK and GCSE, IB teaching. We also give HSK level classification which will give you a cross reference for your Chinese standard. Many students call it "LIFE SAVING" for their exam. It takes our years' painful effort to edit. Thanks for your support for us creating better contents for you!

How to use these course effectively?

- Intensive Revision PDF Book will be used as Textbook.
- Online Quiz – will enable student to access their own progress.
- Intensive Revision Video Course - the in-depth explanation by our expert teachers in video will serve as virtual teacher for students.

David YAO, Founder of

www.Edeo.biz   &   www.legoomandarin.com

26 April 2019

About the Author:

David Yao, the founder of www.LegooMandarin.com and Educational Video Courses Online (www.Edeo.biz), born in china, resides in Kuala Lumpur, Malaysia, holding Master degree from University Malaya, has 25 years' experience in mandarin teaching for foreigners, creating a SYSTEM (more than 200 mandarin courses) designed for foreigners to study Chinese as secondary language. He practices Tai Chi for almost 30 years and establishes Tai Chi Fitness Organization (http://taichifitness.org/) to modernize and promote Tai Chi for fitness and health.

Scan QR code for Lifetime Access to Full Video course together with this book

@ the best price in Udemy:

QRcode-pro.com

Our Story

"Share with You What We Know Best" is our Slogan. We start with LEGOO Mandarin and now expand the system into other topics: Bahasa Malaysia, IT eCommerce, Accounting and Finance, Tai Chi Fitness and Qi Gong. You can learn anytime anywhere!

In addition to be a **Contents Provider**, we also provide **Online Systems,** which can be easily integrated with your school or company online system or use separately. We are using Udemy and other more than 10 similar platforms for video courses marketing. The Amazon KDP, Google Books and Apple iBooks are platforms we publishing our textbooks in addition to our own platform. We provide consultancy service to save your time and give you the best tips on how to leverage your efforts using all these amazing platforms. Please contact us for quotations (very reasonable price).

We can assign our trained teachers to conduct **live lesson** through Webinar, Skype and YouTube, Facebook at reasonable price.

Licencing Program to schools & Resellers

We offer Licencing Program to schools! More schools are using our system! You can use quiz, video course, PPT and PDF under our Licencing Program. Customized course development with your own LOGO can be done. Please contact us for details and quotations (very reasonable price).

Licencing Program to Resellers
We offer Licencing Program to Resellers, book stores and other Platforms (Websites, Google stores, Groupons, Facebook stores). We provide contents such PDF books, online Quiz and Video Courses. You can list our contents in your platform. We will share on 50-50 sales basis. We can provide technical assistance to integrate our contents with your system and help response within 24 hours.

Please contact us by whatsapp +60163863716.

David Yao Amazon Kindle Author Central page

For Hardcopy or paperback books at best price with reduced postage,
please visit: David Yao Amazon Kindle Author Central page:

http://bit.ly/david-amazon-kdp (USA)

https://www.amazon.co.uk/-/e/B07PR3LTMQ (UK)

https://www.amazon.de/-/e/B07PR3LTMQ (German)

http://www.amazon.fr/-/e/B07PR3LTMQ (France)

https://www.amazon.co.jp/~/e/B07PR3LTMQ (Japan)

https://www.amazon.com/-/e/B07PR3LTMQ (USA)

Pearson Edexcel GCSE In Chinese (5CN03/3F) Paper 3F Foundation Tier Reading and Understanding in Chinese

Q1 Match Chinese Characters with Picture (Meaning).

1 Here are some of David's belongings.

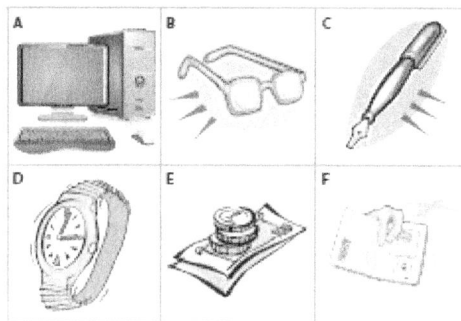

眼镜

钱

手表

护照

笔

(Total for Question 1 = 4 marks)

Examination Skills:
Remember the key words.

眼镜

钱

手表

护照

笔

Vocabulary Builder and Expansion:
词汇解释及词汇扩展

眼镜	yǎnjìng	(名[1]) glasses; spectacles	HSK 3 new
太阳眼镜	tàiyáng yǎnjìng	Sunglasses	
眼睛	yǎnjīng	(名) eye	HSK 2 new
钱	qián	(名) money	
钱包	qiánbāo	(名) purse; wallet	
手表	shǒubiǎo	(名) wristwatch	
护照	hùzhào	(名) passport:	HSK 3 new
笔	bǐ	(名) pen; (any writing tools similar to pen)	
圆珠笔	yuánzhūbǐ	(名) ballpoint pen	

---

[1](名) indicates 名词 míngcí   Noun

Q2 Match the statements with the correct weather conditions.

2. Weather A group of friends describe their plans for different weather conditions.

Match the statements with the correct weather conditions.

2 Weather A group of friends describe their plans for different weather
conditions.
Match the statements with the correct weather conditions.

今天很冷，我要穿毛衣。
冬天下大雪，我要去滑雪。
夏天很热，我要去游泳。
秋天风大，我要去放风筝。
春天多雨，我要穿雨衣。

(Total for Question 2 = 4 marks)

▸ A hot

▸ B raining

▸ C cloudy

▸ D snowing

▸ E windy

▸ F cold

A hot   B raining   C cloudy   D snowing E windy   F cold

今天很冷，我要穿毛衣。

冬天下大雪，我要去滑雪。

夏天很热，我要去游泳。

秋天风大，我要去放风筝。

春天多雨，我要穿雨衣。

(Total for Question 2 = 4 marks)

The Correct Answer

T_EXT

▸ 2 Weather A group of friends describe their plans for different weather conditions.

▸ Match the statements with the correct weather conditions.

▸ 今天很冷，我要穿毛衣。
▸ 冬天下大雪，我要去滑雪。
▸ 夏天很热，我要去游泳。
▸ 秋天风大，我要去放风筝。
▸ 春天多雨，我要穿雨衣。

▸ (Total for Question 2 = 4 marks)

A hot

B raining

C cloudy

D snowing

E windy

F cold

Examination Skills:

Find the key words. Guess if you don't know.

今天很冷，我要穿毛衣。

It's cold today, I want to wear a sweater.

冬天下大雪，我要去滑雪。

It's snowing heavily in winter, I'm going to ski.

夏天很热，我要去游泳。

It's very hot in summer, I want to go swimming.

秋天风大，我要去放风筝。

It's windy in autumn, I'm going to fly a kite.

春天多雨，我要穿雨衣。

It's rainy in spring, I want to wear a raincoat.

Vocabulary Builder and Expansion:
词汇解释及词汇扩展

冷　　lěng　　　　(形) cold:　　　　　　　　HSK 1　new

毛衣　máoyī　　　(名) woollen sweater; Jumpers

冬天　dōngtiān　　(名) winter

雪　　xuě　　　　(名) snow

下雪　xià xuě　　snowing

昨天下了一场大雪。

zuótiān xiàle yī chǎng dàxuě.

It snowed heavily yesterday

滑雪　　　huáxuě　　(名) skiing (动) to ski

夏天　　　xiàtiān　　(名) summar

热　　　　rè　　　　(形[2]) hot:　　　　　　　HSK 1　new

游泳　　　yóuyǒng　(动[3]) swim:　　　　　　HSK 2　new

秋天　　　qiūtiān　　(名) autumn

风筝　　　fēngzhēng　(名) kite:

――――――――――――――――

[2] (形) indicates 形容词　xíngróngcí　　　Adjective

[3] (动) indicates 动词　dòngcí　　　Verb

放风筝	fàng fēngzhēng	(动) fly a kite
春天	chūntiān	(名) spring
雨衣	yǔyī	(名) raincoat

Q3 Match the Sentences with the Location indicated

Places to go

3 Where should each person go?

Places to go
3 Where should each person go?

A 美美要买一份英文报纸。
B 大伟想和家人一起去看
足球比赛。
C 王勇想买一个照相机。
D 明明要买火车票去北京。
E 丽丽想和同学一起去看
国画展览。
F 马田想买一杯咖啡。

Match the correct letter to the location

1 department store

2 newsagent

3 coffee shop

4 ticket office

5 art gallery

6 stadium

(Total for Question 3 = 4 marks)

A 美美要买一份英文报纸。

B 大伟想和家人一起去看足球比赛。

C 王勇想买一个照相机。

D 明明要买火车票去北京。

E 丽丽想和同学一起去看国画展览。

F 马田想买一杯咖啡。

Match the correct letter to the location

Example: department store

(i) newsagent

(ii) coffee shop

(iii) ticket office

(iv) art gallery

(Total for Question 3 = 4 marks)

Examination Skills & Explanations:

A 美美要买一份英文报纸。

A Meimei wants to buy an English newspaper.

B 大伟想和家人一起去看足球比赛。

B Dawei wants to watch a football match with his family.

C 王勇想买一个照相机。

C Wang Yong wants to buy a camera.

D 明明要买火车票去北京。

D obviously wants to buy a train ticket to Beijing.

E 丽丽想和同学一起去看国画展览。

E Lili wants to go to the exhibition of Chinese painting with her classmates.

F 马田想买一杯咖啡。   F Martin wants to buy a cup of coffee.

The Correct Answer:

TEXT   Edexcel GCSE Chinese (5CN03) Intensive Revision Course 历年考卷快送

▸ Places to go
▸ 3 Where should each person go?

▸ A 美美要买一份英文报纸。
▸ B 大伟想和家人一起去看
   足球比赛。
▸ C 王勇想买一个照相机。
▸ D 明明要买火车票去北京。
▸ E 丽丽想和同学一起去看
   国画展览。
▸ F 马田想买一杯咖啡。

▸ Match the correct letter to the location

▸ 1 department store
▸ 2 newsagent
▸ 3 coffee shop
▸ 4 ticket office
▸ 5 art gallery
▸ 6 stadium
▸ (Total for Question 3 = 4 marks)

4

Vocabulary Builder and Expansion:
词汇解释及词汇扩展

报纸	bàozhǐ	(名)newspaper	HSK 2 new
比赛	bǐsài	(名)(动) match; competition	HSK 3 new
足球比赛	zúqiú bǐsài	(名) football match.	
体育馆	tǐyùguǎn	gymnasium; stadium	
照相	zhàoxiàng	take a photo; have a photo taken	
照相机	zhàoxiàngjī	(名) camera	HSK 3 new
火车	huǒchē	(名) train:	
火车票	huǒchē piào	railway ticket.	
国画	guó huà	(名) traditional Chinese painting	
展览	zhǎnlǎn	1 (动) put on display; exhibit; show	HSK 5 new
展览	zhǎnlǎn	2 (名) diplay; exhibition; show:	
咖啡	kāfēi	(名) coffee:	HSK 2 new
咖啡馆	kāfēi guǎn	(名) café.	

报摊	bào tān	news stand	
报社	bàoshè	newspaper office; newspaper press	HSK 6 new
售票处	shòupiào chù	(名) ticket office; booking office	
画廊	huàláng	(picture) gallery	

Q4 Read a short passage in Chinese, then Choose the correct answer in English

My work

4 The following passage describes my daily routine and future plans. (Total for Question 1 = 4 marks)

每天早上我七点起床，去打太极拳，八点吃早餐。我喜欢喝牛奶、吃鸡蛋和水果。八点半，我坐地铁去博物馆上班。我在博物馆工作了四年。现在我想在银行工作，当银行经理。

1 What time do I get up?

A 7.00am   B 7.30am   C 8.00am

(i) What do I like to drink with my breakfast?

A water   B milk   C tea

2 (ii) How do I travel to work?

A bicycle   B car C underground

3 (iii) Where do I work?

A museum   B school   C shopping centre

4 (iv) What job would I like to do?

A bank manager   B sports teacher   C scientist

(Total for Question 4 = 4 marks)

The Correct Answer

TEXT

▶ My work   4 The following passage describes my daily routine and future plans. (Total for Question 1 = 4 marks)

▶ 每天早上我七点起床，去打太极拳，八点吃早餐。我喜欢喝牛奶、吃鸡蛋和水果。八点半，我坐地铁去博物馆上班。我在博物馆工作了四年。现在我想在银行工作，当银行经理。

▶ 1 What time do I get up?

▶ ✓ 7.00am   B 7.30am   C 8.00am

▶ (i) What do I like to drink with my breakfast?

▶ A water   B ✓ milk   C tea

▶ 2 (ii) How do I travel to work?

▶ A bicycle   B car   ✓ underground

▶ 3 (iii) Where do I work?

▶ ✓ museum   B school   C shopping centre

▶ 4 (iv) What job would I like to do?

▶ ✓ bank manager   B sports teacher   C scientist

4

Examination Skills & Explanations:

每天早上我七点起床，去打太极拳，

八点吃早餐。

我喜欢喝牛奶、吃鸡蛋和水果。

八点半，我坐地铁去博物馆上班。

我在博物馆工作了四年。

现在我想在银行工作，当银行经理。

Měitiān zǎoshang wǒ qī diǎn qǐchuáng, qù dǎ tàijí quán,

 bā diǎn chī zǎocān.

Wǒ xǐhuān hē niúnǎi, chī jīdàn hé shuǐguǒ.

Bā diǎn bàn, wǒ zuò dìtiě qù bówùguǎn shàngbān.

Wǒ zài bówùguǎn gōngzuòle sì nián.

 Xiànzài wǒ xiǎng zài yínháng gōngzuò, dāng yínháng jīnglǐ.

Every morning I get up at seven, go to Tai Chi, and have breakfast at eight. I like to drink milk, eat eggs and fruits. At half past eight, I took the subway to go to work in the museum. I have worked in the museum for four years.
Now I want to work in a bank as a bank manager.

Vocabulary Builder and Expansion:
词汇解释及词汇扩展

起床	qǐchuáng	(动) get up (from bed)	HSK 2 new
打拳	dǎquán	practice shadow boxing	
太极拳	tàijí quán	Taijiquan; Tai Chi; Shadowboxing	HSK 5 new
打太极拳	dǎ tàijí quán do taiji (shadow boxing).		
早餐	zǎocān	(名) breakfast	HSK 5 YAO
牛奶	niúnǎi	(名) milk	HSK 2 new
地铁	dìtiě	Subway 1	HSK 3 new
博物馆	bówùguǎn	museum:	HSK 5 new
工作	gōngzuò	1[4] (名) work; job:	HSK 1 new
工作	gōngzuò	2 (动) work:	

[4] The number 1 here indicates the First meaning. One Chines Character may have many meanings. A phrase can related to many meanings. This is the hard part of Chinese language. So, pay attention to the Shape of Chinese Characters, at least you can read out or know the meaning, will help you a lot in your Chinese learning journey. i.e 请   qǐng   1 (动) treat

请客   qǐngkè   play the host; stand treat

请   qǐng   2 (敬) please:

请坐   qǐng zuò(动) Please sit; Please take a seat

请   qǐng   hire

聘请   pìnqǐng   (动) invite; hire

请   Qǐng   3.(招待; 款待) entertain

我们请朋友吃午饭。   wǒmen qǐng péngyǒu chī wǔfàn.   we entertained friends to lunch.

请   Qǐng   4.[敬] (用于希望对方做某事) please

请安静。   qǐng ānjìng.   be quiet, please.

银行　　　　yínháng　　（名）bank

上班　　　　shàngbān　　（动）go to work; start work; be on duty HSK 2
new

经理　　　　jīnglǐ 2 (名) manager; director　　　　　　HSK 3 new

Q5 Read a short passage in Chinese, then match the correct answer in English

Favorite pastimes

5   A group of friends describe what they like to do in their free time.

A 大勇：　我喜欢看杂志。

B 马田：　我喜欢玩电子游戏。

C 美美：　我喜欢在电影院看电影。

D 东东：　我喜欢在公园打篮球。

E 丽丽：　我喜欢上网听音乐。

Match the item to the person.

(i) play electronic games

(ii) listen to music

(iii) play basketball

(iv) watch films

(Total for Question 5 = 4 marks)

The Correct Answer

TEXT

- Favourite pastimes
- 5 A group of friends describe what they like to do in their free time.
- A 大勇： 我喜欢看杂志。

- B 马田： 我喜欢玩电子游戏。
- C 美美： 我喜欢在电影院看电影。
- D 东东： 我喜欢在公园打篮球。

- E 丽丽： 我喜欢上网听音乐。

- Match the item to the person.

- (i) play electronic games

- (ii) listen to music

- (iii) play basketball

- (iv) watch films

- (v) read magazine

- (Total for Question 5 = 4 marks)

3

Examination Skills & Explanations:

A 大勇： 我喜欢看杂志。

A dàyǒng: Wǒ xǐhuān kàn zázhì.

A Dayong: I like to read magazines.

B 马田： 我喜欢玩电子游戏。

B mǎ tián: Wǒ xǐhuān wán diànzǐ yóuxì.

B Martin: I like playing video games.

C 美美： 我喜欢在电影院看电影。

C měiměi: Wǒ xǐhuān zài diànyǐngyuàn kàn diànyǐng.

C Meimei: I like to watch movies in the cinema.

D 东东： 我喜欢在公园打篮球。

D dōng dōng: Wǒ xǐhuān zài gōngyuán dǎ lánqiú.

D Dongdong: I like playing basketball in the park.

E 丽丽： 我喜欢上网听音乐。

E lì lì: Wǒ xǐhuān shàngwǎng tīng yīnyuè

E Lili: I like to listen to music online.

Vocabulary Builder and Expansion:
词汇解释及词汇扩展

杂志	zázhì	(名) magazine	HSK 4 new
游戏	yóuxì	(名) recreation; game	HSK 3 new
游戏机	yóuxì jī	(名) video game player; TV game player	
电子游戏	diànzǐ yóuxì	Electronic games	
电动游戏	diàndòng yóuxì	Video game	
篮球	lánqiú	(名) basketball:	
篮球场	lánqiú chǎng	basketball court.	
篮球队	lánqiú duì	basketball team	
打篮球	dǎ lánqiú	play basketball.	

音乐	yīnyuè	(名) music:	HSK 3 new
音乐会	yīnyuè huì	(名) concert.	
音乐家	yīnyuè jiā	musician	
流行音乐	liúxíng yīnyuè	popular music	
听音乐	tīng yīnyuè	listen to music	

Q6 Read a short passage in Chinese, then match the correct answer in English

Weekend

6 What does my family do at the weekend?

A 哥哥在图书馆看书。

B 妹妹在床上睡觉。

C 弟弟在花园里踢足球。

D 姐姐在书房里写电子邮件。

E 爸爸在厨房做饭。

F 妈妈在学习开车。

Example: learning to drive F

(i) cooking

(ii) reading

(iii) playing football

(iv) sleeping

(Total for Question 6 = 4 marks)

Examination Skills & Explanations:

A 哥哥在图书馆看书。

A Elder brother is reading books in the library.

A gēgē zài túshū guǎn kànshū.

B 妹妹在床上睡觉。

B Sister is sleeping on the bed.

B mèimei zài chuángshàng shuìjiào.

C 弟弟在花园里踢足球。

C Younger brother is playing football in the garden.

C dìdì zài huāyuán lǐ tī zúqiú.

D 姐姐在书房里写电子邮件。

D Elder sister is writing emails in the study room.

D jiějiě zài shūfáng lǐ xiě diànzǐ yóujiàn.

E 爸爸在厨房做饭。

E Dad is cooking in the kitchen.

E bàba zài chúfáng zuò fàn.

F 妈妈在学习开车。

F Mom is learning drive. F māmā zài xuéxí kāichē.

The Correct Answer

T_{EXT}   Edexcel GCSE Chinese (5CN03) Intensive Revision Course 历年考卷快送

- Weekend
- 6 What does my family do at the weekend?
- A 哥哥在图书馆看书。
- B 妹妹在床上睡觉。
- C 弟弟在花园里踢足球。
- D 姐姐在书房里写电子邮件。
- E 爸爸在厨房做饭。
- F 妈妈在学习开车。

1 learning to drive
2 cooking
3 reading
4 playing football
5 sleeping
6 reply email

3

Vocabulary Builder and Expansion:
词汇解释及词汇扩展

图书馆　　　túshū guǎn　（名）library

踢足球　　　tī zúqiú　　（动）play football

书房　　　　shūfáng　　　study room

她在书房看书。

tā zài shūfáng kànshū.

She is reading in the study room.

电子邮件　　diànzǐ yóujiàn　　（名）E-mail

厨房　　　　chúfáng　　（名）kitchen:

开车　　　　kāichē　　　1（动）drive or start a car, train. etc.

Q7 Read a short passage in Chinese, then choose the Phrase to finish the sentence in English

Lili and Anna

7 The following passage is about Lili and Anna.

Read the text and write the correct letter to complete the sentences.

上个月，丽丽和安娜开始上中学，每天都要骑自行车去上学。丽丽有一辆蓝色的自行车，安娜的是红色的。每个星期六，丽丽骑自行车到美术馆学习画画。但是，安娜喜欢到河边去跑步。星期天晚上，丽丽喜欢去跳舞。安娜喜欢和朋友去唱歌。

Write the correct letter in the box.

Example: Anna and Lili get to school by… A

(i) Every Saturday Lili studies…

(ii) By the river, Anna likes…

(iii) On Sunday evening Lili likes…

(iv) Anna and her friends like to go…

(Total for Question 7 = 4 marks)

A Cycling   B jogging   C walking   D dancing   E painting   F singing

Examination Skills & Explanations:

上个月，丽丽和安娜开始上中学，

每天都要骑自行车去上学。

丽丽有一辆蓝色的自行车，安娜的是红色的。

每个星期六，丽丽骑自行车到美术馆学习画画。

但是，安娜喜欢到河边去跑步。

星期天晚上，丽丽喜欢去跳舞。

安娜喜欢和朋友去唱歌。

Shàng gè yuè, lì lì hé ānnà kāishǐ shàng zhōngxué,

měitiān dū yào qí zìxíngchē qù shàngxué.

Lì lì yǒuyī liàng lán sè de zìxíngchē, ānnà de shì hóngsè de.

 Měi gè xīngqíliù, lì lì qí zìxíngchē dào měishù guǎn xuéxí huà huà.

Dànshì, ānnà xǐhuān dào hé biān qù pǎobù.

Xīngqítiān wǎnshàng, lì lì xǐhuān qù tiàowǔ.

Ānnà xǐhuān hé péngyǒu qù chànggē.

Last month, Lili and Anna started to go to middle school,

I have to ride a bicycle to school every day.

Lili has a blue bicycle and Anna's is red.

 Every Saturday, Lili rides a bicycle to the art gallery to learn painting.

However, Anna likes to go for a run by the river.

Lili likes to go dancing on Sunday night.

Anna likes to sing with friends.

The Correct Answer

TEXT

7 The following passage is about Lili and Anna. 上个月，丽丽和安娜开始上中学，每天都要骑自行车去上学。丽丽有一辆蓝色的自行车，安娜的是红色的。每个星期六，丽丽骑自行车到美术馆学习画画。但是，安娜喜欢到河边去跑步。星期天晚上，丽丽喜欢去跳舞。安娜喜欢和朋友去唱歌。

1 Anna and Lili get to school by…

2 Every Saturday Lili studies…

3 By the river, Anna likes…

4 On Sunday evening Lili likes…

5 Anna and her friends like to go…

A cycling

B jogging

C walking

D dancing

E painting

F singing

6

Vocabulary Builder and Expansion:

词汇解释及词汇扩展

骑车	qí chē	(动) ride a bicycle
骑自行车	qí zìxíngchē	(动) ride a bicycle
骑单车	qí dānchē	(动) ride a bicycle

博物馆	bówùguǎn	museum
展览馆	zhǎnlǎn guǎn	exhibition hall.
美术馆	měishù guǎn	art gallery
体育馆	tǐyùguǎn	gymnasium; stadium

海边	hǎibiān	(名) seaside
河边	hé biān	(名) riverside
跑步	pǎobù	(动) run; jog
跑步机	Pǎobù jī	Treadmill

跳舞	tiàowǔ	dance

Q8A Read short sentence in Chinese about Occupations, then match the correct answer in English

Occupations

8A group of friends are describing their occupations.

A 我是护士，在医院工作。

B 我是工程师，在工厂工作。

C 我是老师，在小学工作。

D 我是司机，在公共汽车公司工作。

E 我是运动员，打网球。

F 我是售货员，在书店工作。

Write the correct letter in each box to match the occupations to the people.

Example: sportsman E

(i) engineer

(ii) nurse

(iii) bus driver

(iv) teacher

(Total for Question 8 = 4 marks)

Examination Skills & Explanations:

A 我是护士，在医院工作。

B 我是工程师，在工厂工作。

C 我是老师，在小学工作。

D 我是司机，在公共汽车公司工作。

E 我是运动员，打网球。

F 我是售货员，在书店工作。

A wǒ shì hùshì, zài yīyuàn gōngzuò.

B wǒ shì gōngchéngshī, zài gōngchǎng gōngzuò.

C wǒ shì lǎoshī, zài xiǎoxué gōngzuò.

D wǒ shì sījī, zài gōnggòng qìchē gōngsī gōngzuò.

E wǒ shì yùndòngyuán, dǎ wǎngqiú.

F wǒ shì shòuhuòyuán, zài shūdiàn gōngzuò.

A I am a nurse and work in a hospital.

B I am an engineer and work in a factory.

C I am a teacher and work in a primary school.

D I am a driver and work in a bus company.

E I am an athlete and play tennis.

F I am a sales clerk and work in a bookstore.

The Correct Answer

TEXT   Edexcel GCSE Chinese (5CN03) Intensive Revision Course 历年考卷快送

▸ 8A group of friends are describing their occupations.

▸ A 我是护士，在医院工作。

▸ B 我是工程师，在工厂工作。

▸ C 我是老师，在小学工作。

▸ D 我是司机，在公共汽车公司工作。

▸ E 我是运动员，打网球。

▸ F 我是售货员，在书店工作。

1 sportsman

2 engineer

3 nurse

▸

4 bus driver

▸

5 teacher

6 Book shop

4

Vocabulary Builder and Expansion:
词汇解释及词汇扩展

护士　　　　hùshì　　　　（名）(hospital) nurse

护理　　　　hùlǐ　　　　（动）nurse; tend:

护理伤病员　hùlǐ shāng bìng yuán　　　nurse the sick and the wounded

医院　　　　yīyuàn　　　（名）hospital:

工程师　　　gōngchéngshī　　　engineer

工厂　　　　gōngchǎng　　　（名）factory; mill ; plant; works

司机　　　　sījī　　　　（名）driver; chauffeur

公司　　　　gōngsī　　　　（名）company; firm; corporation

售货员　　　shòuhuòyuán　　　（名）shop assistant; salesclerk :

售票员　　　shòupiàoyuán　　　（名）ticket seller; (of a bus) conductor; (of a railway station or airport) booking-office clerk; (of a theatre) box-office clerk

Q9 Match basic Chinese phrase and their English meaning! Easy pizzy!

In a house

9 Here are some items that can be found in a house.

A B C D E

Match the pictures to the correct items.

Put a cross in the correct box.

(i) 沙发

(ii) 电视

(iii) 桌子

(iv) 钟

(Total for Question 9 = 4 marks)

The Correct Answer

TEXT   Edexcel GCSE Chinese (5CN03) Intensive Revision Course 历年考卷快送

▸ Match the word with meaning

沙发 ————————————→ ▸ Sofa

▸ Table

▸ dining table

电视 ————————————→ ▸ writing desk

▸ clock

桌子 ————————————→ ▸ alarm clock

钟 ————————————→ ▸ TV

5

Examination Skills:

This is unbelievable easy! The skill is to draw line properly!

Easy peasy lemon squeezy!

Vocabulary Builder and Expansion:
词汇解释及词汇扩展

沙发	shāfā	(名) sofa
电视	diànshì	(名) television; TV:
桌	zhuō	(名) table; desk:
餐桌	cānzhuō	(名) dining table.
饭桌	fànzhuō	(名) dining table.
书桌	shūzhuō	(名) writing desk
钟	zhōng	(名) clock:
闹钟	nào zhōng	(名) alarm clock

Q10 Read a VERY short passage in Chinese, then answer questions in English.-- easy peasy lemon squeezy!

A visit

10 This is a story about Ma Tian.

上个星期，马田去看他的朋友，他朋友住在山上。山上有很多黄色的花儿。他有很多宠物，有小狗、小猫、马和小牛。

Answer the following questions in English.

(a) Who did Ma Tian go to visit? (1)

....

(b) Where is this person's house? (1)

....

(c) What colour are the flowers? (1)

....

(d) What pets does he have? Give one detail. (1)

....

(Total for Question 10 = 4 marks)

TOTAL FOR PAPER: 40 MARKS

Examination Skills & Explanations:

上个星期，马田去看他的朋友，他朋友住在山上。山
上有很多黄色的花儿。他有很多宠物，有小狗、小猫、
马和小牛。

Shàng gè xīngqí, mǎ tián qù kàn tā de péngyǒu, tā péngyǒu zhù zài
shānshàng. Shānshàng yǒu hěnduō huángsè de huā er. Tā yǒu hěnduō
chǒngwù, yǒu xiǎo gǒu, xiǎo māo, mǎ hé xiǎo niú.

Last week, Martin went to see his friend, who lives in the mountains. There
are many yellow flowers on the mountain. He has many pets, including
puppies, kittens, horses and calves.

The Correct Answer

Answer the following questions in English.

(a) Who did Ma Tian go to visit? (1)

看他的朋友 visit his friend

(b) Where is this person's house? (1)

在山上 In the mountains

(c) What colour are the flowers? (1)

黄色的花儿 Yellow flower

(d) What pets does he have? Give one detail. (1)

小狗、 小猫、 马和小牛。 Puppies, kittens, horses and calves.

Examination Skills:

This is GCSE, answer in English. In IGCSE, you are required to answer in Chinese. (You can copy and paste, but sometime harder to find what to copy.) But here you should know the meaning of Chinese Characters.

The vocabulary here is so EASY! Good for you.

See Edexcel GCSE / IGCSE (4CN, 5CN03F, 5CN03H) Classified Chinese Vocabulary Book V2019 http://edeo.biz/6553, your LIFE SAVING BOOK! Use "youtube30" to have 30% OFF!

Vocabulary Builder and Expansion:
词汇解释及词汇扩展

住	zhù	(动) live; reside; stay
黄色	huángsè	(名) yellow
宠物	chǒngwù	(名) pet

Printed in Great Britain
by Amazon